Unforgiveness
Let It Go Or Die With It

Gemettte McEachern

Cover Design: Premier BMS
Editor: Rain Publishing
Interior Layout & Formatting: Purposely Booked

For more information please visit theleadinggem.com.

IBSN 978-1-7369023-0-1 (Paper)

IBSN 978-1-7369023-1-8 (eBook)

Dedication

This book is dedicated to you, Daddy. When I was a child, I loved watching you cut grass. When it would get too hot outside, I knew before you would ask that you needed a cold glass of ice water. I would have never thought that the same girl who carried the cold glass of water would become ICE COLD towards you one day. I thank God that you did not give up on me, even in my wrong. I dedicate this book to you!

Love Beyond Expression,

Gemette

A Special Note

Erin and Victor,

I want you to know that I love you so much! It is my deepest desire that I do not pass any of my flaws to you. I want you to learn from the mistakes of your mother. When people make you angry, and they will, let this book help you deal with your emotions. Trust God and pray he will help you get through any situation with family, friends, co-workers, church members, and your spouse. Remember to love people for who they are. Do not seek revenge because it will come with a cost.

Love Always,

Mommie

About the Author

Gemette LaShawn McEachern loves her role as a beacon of faith and as an educator, speaker, and author. She strives to bring the word of God to those in need of faith and renew faith for all who hear her words. Gemette is a member of New Light, where she serves as First Lady, and she is always looking for new ways to serve her community. With an Undergraduate and Master's degree at Fayetteville State University and a Master of School Administration from UNC Pembroke, she is dedicated to education.

Gemette lives in Fayetteville, North Carolina, with her husband, Pastor Victor McEachern, their two beautiful children, Erin and Victor, and their German Shepherd, Prophet. When she is not busy as a wife and mother, or working within her community, she enjoys singing, dancing, and planning events. Her desire to lift Christian women into leadership roles shines through in her work as a speaker. She believes that this book is one of the many ways God has guided her to help make a difference, both in her family and her community. She hopes to teach others that through God, anything is possible.

Table of Contents

Foreword
by Victor McEachern

Watching this book come to fruition has been an emotional rollercoaster for me. At times I have been saddened by the memory of long nights filled with tears and frustration. I remember feeling completely helpless as I watched my best friend struggle with problems she was too ill-equipped to handle. On many occasions, I chose not to bombard her with scriptures she already knew but rather be the shoulder, ear, and friend she needed. At other times, we laughed and joked about the kind of things that only seem funny in hindsight, which, in my opinion, is a sign that true healing has taken place. But it didn't just stir up feelings of grief and joy; there was amazement. I was completely amazed at just how far The Lord has brought her (us). I can honestly say she is not the same fractured church girl I met over twenty years ago. She is the whole and healed woman of God I married.

I believe this book is a gift to the Body of Christ. Tragically, it seems that many Christians have chosen to live in unforgiveness versus going through the sometimes-difficult process of forgiving those who harmed them.

Forgiveness is one of God's non-negotiables, and without it, there is no path forward with Him. Still, it is almost unimaginable to think that as long as we hold unforgiveness towards our brother or sister, God withholds His forgiveness from us (see Matthew 18:22-35). So, consider this book as God's way to get you unstuck. Please don't regard this hallowed moment as a mere coincidence. Unforgiveness: Let It Go or Die with It has come at exactly the right time. God is pouring out His Grace and Mercy in these last days, and He doesn't want you to miss it. My sincere prayer is that if you see yourself within pages of this book, you won't allow yourself to rest until you "Let It Go" so you don't have to "Die with It."

Introduction

"I'm sorry, but you're going to have to let it go," he said without breaking eye contact. "Forgive, bury the hatchet, and walk in love. If you don't, it's going to come back to haunt you! Gemette, I'm serious as a heart attack. You'll see this again."

His words felt like little, prickly needles sticking in the back of my neck. It's not that I hadn't heard those words before; it is just that they usually applied to something more frivolous like puppy love gone wrong or an argument that I hadn't won yet. No matter what the situation had been, I always left Pastor Goings' office admitting that I may have possibly played a small part in whatever I was mad about at the time, which made his advice a bit more palatable.

This time was a little different. No, a lot different! I was completely innocent. I had absolutely nothing to do with it. In fact, it didn't even happen to me; it happened to someone I loved.

"Why do I have to forgive, bury the hatchet, and walk in love?" I sat there, backtalking and sassing like a little kid (at least in my mind) while trying not to show it on my face. I failed miserably. That session was different, but not only because of my innocence, but it was also different because of his warning, "If you don't, it's going to come back to haunt you."

This book is dedicated to the thing that came back to "haunt me." I will share with you the battle I fought with unforgiveness and its effects on my marriage, children, relationships, career, and ultimately, my health. I pray that you read this book as more than a cautionary tale. It has been written with you in mind. It is my prayer that you not only see the mistakes I've made, but you discover the mistakes you may be making yourself. We all have blindspots, so let this book serve as a side-view mirror for your life. I have included a few questions at the end of each chapter, along with some scriptures for reflection. Please feel free to use the space to record your answers and make sure you read and apply the scriptures to your everyday life.

"To forgive is to set a prisoner free and discover the prisoner was you." - Lewis B. Smedes

SIGNS THAT YOU HAVE NOT FORGIVEN CHECKLIST

Answer the questions below:

 Does the memory of an offense continue to remain fresh in your mind?

 Have you maintained negative emotions toward the person(s) who offend you?

 Do you feel comfortable in the presence of the person who offended you?

 Is revenge your ultimate goal?

If you said yes to any of the questions above, grab your favorite pen and highlighter.

I encourage you to apply the words and the advice that will be shared within the pages of this book. I pray that your life will never be the same. Let the healing begin!

"You will always have an area of your life that needs to be healed. Becoming more like Jesus is a lifetime process."

Chapter 1
It's Not My Problem

"This is what the LORD says to you: Do not be afraid or discouraged because of this vast army. For the battle is not yours, but God's.... Go out to face them tomorrow, and the LORD will be with you." - 2 Chronicles 20:15-NIV

Raised by both parents in the church, we had a beautiful family. We possessed deep love and respect for each other and for those who came to our house. We were all thrilled about having our monthly family meetings. During our time together, my father taught us the word of God. He also used that time to bring correction and address certain family matters. Those meetings strengthened our bond, and we were convinced that "a family that prayed together stayed together."

Who would have thought that my parents would divorce after twenty-seven years of marriage? Surely if they made it that long, they could make it until death. However, that was not the case. My father was a minister and faithful to his church and family. He knew the Word of God and taught us to believe every word that came from the Bible. My father preached at home before he preached in the pulpit. He lived the life before us, which is why every time he went to preach at a local church, I was there singing before he brought forth the word.

I thought that my parents' marriage was untouchable. They were in love for the most part, but soon I discovered that no words, tears, or even kids could keep them together. Anyway, this is not my problem, but keep reading, and I will show you how it became a problem for me.

One day I entered the threshold of the door to our house and heard sobs and sniffles coming from my mom's bedroom. As I rushed in to see what was going on, there was my mom, sitting upright, holding her teary face in her hands. My dad was pacing the floor, saying, "I am done, I am done." My eyes captured an essay typed by my mom and a bowl of ramen noodles spilled all over the floor. My mom was sobbing hysterically, crying, "He destroyed my paper!" She had been working hard on becoming a National Board-Certified Teacher, and all her work had noodles on it. Suddenly, a rushing wave of anger came over me. This would be the first time that I stood up to the man I used to give ice water to before he would even ask. I yelled as loud as I could, "Why did you do that? She didn't do anything to you." I was so angry that I wanted to throw a cinderblock in the front windshield of his new car - the same new car that my mom and neighbor found him and another woman in just months before. It felt as if my heart was beating violently against my ribcage.

The pain didn't stop there. Valentine's Day rolled around, and my father decided to bring home the gift his girlfriend purchased. He and my mother were not on good terms, and instead of trying to mend the relationship, he further destroyed it. There was a white monogrammed towel set with a teddy bear on top. The teddy bear was holding a red helium balloon. He did not hide the gift; he boldly left it on the bathroom counter so that my mother could see it. How could he be so cruel?

I remember having to call my Pastor to calm me down. In my mind, I had every right to be angry at my dad. In my twenty-three years of living, I had never experienced such drama. That night, I gave birth to the spirit of anger and unforgiveness. I had no words my dad, and I never wanted to see or talk to him again. He finally moved out, and it was the best thing because I remember being up at night plotting on how I could get him back for the pain I saw in my mother's eyes. Our relationship was never the same.

I now realize that I gave birth to something that was NOT MY PROBLEM. You will always have an area of your life that needs to be healed. Becoming more like Jesus is a lifetime process, and there are many things that we need God's help to fix. The Bible says, "the earth is the Lord's and the fullness thereof - the world and they that dwell therein" Psalms 24:1. God is in charge of everything. I want you to take a moment and reflect on that person who has offended you. Maybe they didn't show up on a special occasion or betrayed your trust. Ask yourself, "Is this my problem?" I had to learn that God does not need my help to correct people or help them to see their wrong. But that is exactly what I tried to do. Let me tap you on the shoulder as the Holy Spirit did to me one day. He whispered, "Let me fix it."

Why do we need to let God fix our problems? Because we cannot fix them on our own! John 15:5 says, "...for without me ye can do nothing." Psychologists generally define forgiveness as a conscious, deliberate decision to release feelings of resentment or vengeance toward a person or group who has harmed you, regardless of whether they deserve your forgiveness or not. So, when we are hurt, it is not our problem! The Bible simply says, "Vengeance is mine, says the Lord" (Romans 12:19). This scripture never crossed my mind when I was holding grudges. I thank God for a second chance to get it right. You can get it right too! You must first be honest with yourself.

Understanding what forgiveness is not, is just as important as defining what forgiveness is. Experts who study or teach forgiveness make it clear that when you forgive, you do not gloss over or deny the seriousness of an offense against you. Forgiveness does not forgetting, nor does it mean condoning or excusing offenses. Though forgiveness can help repair a damaged relationship, it doesn't obligate you to reconcile with the person who harmed you or release them from legal accountability.

Instead, forgiveness brings the forgiver peace of mind and

frees him or her from corrosive anger. While there is some debate over whether true forgiveness requires positive feelings toward the offender, experts agree that forgiveness at least involves letting go of deeply held negative feelings. In that way, it empowers you to recognize the pain you've suffered without letting that pain define you, enabling you to heal and move on with your life.

Reflection of Chapter 1
It's Not my Problem

Please feel free to write your response below or in a journal.
Ask yourself the following questions:
Who are you upset with?

_____

_____

_____

_____

_____

_____

_____

_____

_____

_____

_____

_____

_____

_____

_____

_____

_____

_____

_____

_____

_____

_____

_____

Why?

How do you feel when they are around you?

Describe what you want to happen. (Be Honest)

Is this your problem?

"When you have made the choice not to forgive a person, and don't deal with it, it turns into bitterness."

Chapter 2
Deal with It!

> "A soft answer turneth away wrath: but grievous words stir up anger. The tongue of the wise useth knowledge aright: but the mouth of fools poureth out foolishness."
> -Proverbs 15:1-2- KJV

The unforgiving spirit that I gave birth to refused to be soothed, it refused to be healed, and it refused to forget. My parents got legally separated, and I was hurt but relieved in a sense. I was happy that my mom was no longer experiencing the pain he caused, but she was still hurting. I often heard her on the phone with my grandmother fussing, crying, and then praying. I knew her love for my father was still there, and it seemed she thought that what she was going through was just a phase, and it would be over soon.

Who would be praying for someone who has emotionally abused them and said they did not want them anymore? Her love was so strong that if he had come through the door and asked her to take him back, she would have. Seeing my mother this way left me with deep trust issues. Although my heart ached for her, I tried my best to cover it up and be strong for her. I had to put the mask on and cover up the fact that I was hurt, angry, disappointed, stressed, embarrassed, and ashamed. I had to face the people at church, in the community, and on my job with the shame of my parents going through a divorce. One of the things that I lived most of my life telling myself and others was, "I am not mad; I am not angry." Every time someone asked me if I was angry, I would quickly say no. When you decide not to forgive a person and refuse to deal with the hurt head-on, that hurt turns into bitterness. I wanted to seek revenge for my dad hurting my family. I had become a religious phony who was bitter to the core.

Let me share an example of how your emotions can get the best of you. My father had purchased a nice used Honda Accord for me after my freshman year in college. After driving it for some years and putting over 300,000 miles on it, it began to give me trouble. One Saturday afternoon, I was having issues with the car and called my dad several times, but he did not pick up his phone. Of course, my mind only went to the presumption that he was with a woman and did not care about me. As my anger grew, the car began to break down; soon, it came to a complete stop in the middle of a busy highway. Thank God we were near a car lot. My mom and I pushed the car to the car dealership, and she said with tears in her eyes, "Let's get you another car." My first thought was, "You don't know how to pick out a car. Daddy is the car person in the family". However, with anger, I proceeded to sign the papers. The interest rate was 23.9%. When I drove the car off the lot, I was happy and felt that I didn't need my daddy anymore. Well, let's just say I paid for this car several times.

Unfortunately, I got into a car accident a few years later and totaled the car. It was not until then that I realized I purchased that car out of anger and resentment. I was upside down in the car and didn't have any GAP insurance. After the insurance company paid for the car, I was even angrier at myself because I could not afford to buy another car and still pay for the one I lost.

You would think that would have gotten my attention, NOPE! It was not until I was trying to pass a Praxis exam after taking it fifteen times did I realize that unforgiveness was attacking me in so many areas in my life. The night before my last try, I remember crying, asking God to help me pass his test?" He did not answer. I struggled. My pride rebelled. "After all that he has done to you and your mom, are you going to call him? You have not talked to him in years." Pride almost won, but I was desperate. I would do anything at that point. I picked up the phone, and his new wife answered. I said, "Can I speak to my dad, and could both of you stay on the phone?" She was shocked; you could hear it in her voice. I said, "I need to ask you to forgive me. I have been treating you guys very badly, and I am sorry. I should not have done that." After that conversation, it was like a one-hundred-pound weight lifted off me. I cried after ending the conversation, praised God, and went to sleep. I took my test the next day, and I passed it! I still cannot believe that I took that test fifteen times and spent hundreds of dollars each time I failed. The Bible says, "The wages of sin is death but the gift of God is eternal life," Romans 6:23. Living in sin will cost you more than you are willing to pay.

It took this Christian woman over five years to forgive her father. After calling him and setting things in order, I began to work on my relationship with him slowly. My mom found love at a funeral, dated for a while, and got married, which caused her to move away. This was truly bittersweet. I was happy for the love she found but sad that it took her to New York. Living alone was a challenge. However, with the help of the Lord and a lump sum of money from my mom, I survived. The healing of my relationship with my dad took place when I came home from work one day, and someone had broken into my house. They went through everything I had. The first person I called was my DADDY. He came over and said, "You are moving! You can come and move in with us until you find somewhere else to live." I was like, "WHAT?!" He even talked to his new wife about the formerly unforgiving daughter moving in with them. I was reluctant and embarrassed because I him so badly. I was afraid to go back into my house, treated so I gave in, and we scheduled a meeting to put some rules in place. I paid $200 a month to live there and assisted with buying food. Where can you live for $200 a month? During this time, the bond between my dad and I began to mend, and I could not believe that I was living with him. We had no issues absolutely none. I enjoyed sitting in the backyard, having small talk with him, and watching TV.

I know that ALL things work together for good. This situation brought to mind the quote that my pastor's wife often used, "Sometimes we can accuse others of being wrong until we end up wrong ourselves." Shortly after that, I began looking for my own place after saving so much money. God blessed me to purchase my own home before getting married.

When we refuse to deal with unforgiveness, we welcome the devil to wreak havoc in our hearts and relationships. Why did it take me so long to deal with my emotions of anger and bitterness?

1. **I told myself time can heal** - Yes, time can heal but, time can also hurt. Holding onto anger and bitterness for too long can prevent you from healing and living abundantly. You must have true confession, correction, repentance, and forgiveness.

2. **Pride** - "Pride goeth before destruction and a haughty spirit before a fall"- Proverbs 16:18

When you get a flat tire, you can change it or put on a spare. The spare is only meant to buy you some time; it is not intended for you to keep riding on it for days. It is the same thing with anger. The Bible says, "Let not the sun go down on your wrath" Ephesian 4:26. You must deal with your anger. I want to share with you a few ways I have dealt with my anger.

1. Check your tone. When I become upset, I can make matters worse by my response to the problem. Proverbs 15:1 "A gentle answer turns away wrath, but a harsh word stirs up anger."

2. You must do the hard thing. HUMBLE yourself.

3. You must own it. Admit you are wrong. Get the focus off the other person. Deal with you!

4. The Bible tells us to seek peace and pursue it. (Psalms 34:14). Turn from evil and do good. Pray and ask God to bring peace.

Reflection of Chapter 2
Deal With It

Please feel free to write your response below or in a journal. Ask yourself the following questions:

Are there any conflicts you need to face but are avoiding? If you answered yes, explain.

Complete the following sentence:
Today I am willing to release all angry thoughts about

_____

_____

_____

_____

_____

_____

_____

_____

_____

_____

How will you deal with the situation? Pray, and if you need to talk to the offender, determine how and when. In person? On the phone? Through a letter?

_____

_____

_____

_____

_____

_____

_____

_____

_____

"Spiritual maturity is achieved through becoming more like Christ."

Chapter 3
"You're too Big for That."

Therefore, let us move beyond the elementary teachings about Christ and be taken forward to maturity, not laying again the foundation of repentance from acts that lead to death, and of faith in God. - Hebrews 6:1-NIV

Thank God I forgave! Thank God I allowed Him to take me through the healing process of letting go of the hurt!

I now wanted to marry this fine, handsome man I ran into during my extended time in college. We dated a while, and for some time, I was not ready for marriage. After nine years, he finally asked me to be his wife. Unforgiveness affected so many areas of my life because my heart was HARD. I didn't want to leave my church to be with my husband, but he was not leaving his church to be with me. Seeing my parent's divorce left me with the fear of getting married. I didn't want what happened to my mother to happen to me. I am not sure I would have responded the same way. After attending counseling, praying, and fasting, the Lord spoke and told me through my Pastor that I would be okay. Thank God I recorded the prophecy because I played it back fifty times before I had peace. When the proposal came, I said, "YES!" We got married on the beautiful island of Ocho Rios, Jamaica. By then, my dad was divorced for the second time, and I had to deal with a new lady at my wedding. However, she was sweet as pie, and because I made a conscious decision to walk in love and forgiveness, I had no room in my heart for bitterness or malice. My father was happy, and so was I. Two years after being married to a Pastor's son, we conceived and gave birth to a beautiful baby girl. We prayed over our daughter every day, and I hoped that she would be better than her mother. God told me that Erin would be my helper. I did not know how she would help me, but she did.

In my second year of marriage, I will never forget the day that my job had a special dinner for the administrative team and their spouses. All the spouses showed up... except mine. I had told him about the dinner and even told him what I wanted him to wear. I waited and waited for him to arrive, but he never came. I called, and he did not pick up his phone. I sat there watching all the other spouses eat and enjoy their lunch, and I had to sit there by myself. It really took me two days to speak to my husband again. I remember sleeping in our guest room to keep from talking to him. He kept talking, and I played the game of ignoring him. Here again, I found myself walking in unforgiveness. It took much prayer for this one because I felt that my husband did not care about me or the fact that I was totally embarrassed. All he cared about at the time was his job and getting enough sleep. Even though he was ready to move forward, I was not. I wanted to get him back for how he made me feel.

When my daughter began to make the transition from training wheels to the big girl bike, she still wanted to keep the training wheels on. I had to tell her several times that she was too big for the bike. Like mother like daughter, I was too big to be acting and responding the way I did when my husband failed to follow through. I was very comfortable with my personality and the woman that I had become. I didn't think I was acting like a child. As I reflected on my behavior when I did not get my way, I saw all my childish ways.

See, after you get saved, every Christian begins the process of spiritual maturity. Spiritual maturity is achieved through becoming like Christ. You change from pleasing yourself to pleasing God.

Here are some ways that you can tell you are an immature Christian:

1. **Not Listening**- Even though you are warned of the Word, you keep doing the same things anyway. For example, I was twenty-five years old, and my Pastor kept telling me to walk in love. "Forgive your daddy." I heard him, but I didn't listen. "My dear brothers and sisters, take note of this: Everyone should be quick to listen, slow to speak, and slow to become angry." James 1:19

2. **Ignoring the Word**- You ignore the Word because it convicts you of wrong. Not only did I ignore the preached Word, but I also ignored the written Word. Ephesians 4:32 says, "Be kind to one another, tenderhearted, forgiving each other, just as God in Christ also has forgiven you."

3. **Causing Division**- Telling other people things to break the peace in the church, in your homes, and your family. When I chose to remain mad at my father, I recall sharing my feelings with people so that others would know the truth about him. I was so wrong. Instead of covering him, I exposed him, and it felt good. However, the result left others mad and angry, and they joined my party, which made me happy. "Let no corrupt communication come out of your mouth, but only such as is good for building up, as fits the occasion, that it may give grace to those who hear." Ephesians 4:29

4. **Lacking control over your mouth**- When people upset you, how much control do you have over your mouth? For me, in my immature season, I would say whatever I wanted to say, and I didn't care who it hurt in the process. However, the Bible says, "Whoever guards his mouth preserves his life; he who opens wide his lips comes to ruin." Proverbs 13:3.

5. Not considering God's feelings- When I am mad, I want people to know, so they won't do it again. I have been

in so many situations that I was more concerned about how I wanted to punish the person that did me wrong that I did not even consider how God felt about my behavior. "But be ye doers of the word, and not hearers only, deceiving your own selves." James 1:22

We must continue to allow the Word to mature us. How do we grow out of this stage? We must renew our minds. Romans 12:2 says to be not conformed to this world but be ye transformed by the renewing of our minds. The Word is so powerful. "The Word of God is living and active and sharper than any two-edged sword and piercing as far as the division of the soul and spirit of both joints and marrow, and able to judge the thoughts and intentions of the heart," Hebrews 4 :12. I remember spending so much time trying to justify why I should not be the one to apologize. However, the more things began to go wrong in my life, the more I would question God. It was a clear indication that my prayers were being hindered. "If I regard iniquity in my heart, the Lord will not hear me," Psalm 66:18.

Reflection of Chapter 3
"You're too Big for That"

Please feel free to write your response below or in a journal. Ask yourself the following questions:

Identify one area in which you need to mature. Be honest with yourself.

_____

_____

_____

_____

_____

_____

_____

_____

_____

_____

_____

_____

_____

_____

_____

_____

_____

Go back and highlight one scripture from this chapter that you are willing to memorize and write below.

_____
_____
_____
_____
_____
_____
_____

What steps will you take to begin maturing in the area you identified?

_____
_____
_____
_____
_____
_____
_____
_____
_____
_____
_____
_____
_____

Reflect: Draw Closer

Pray and consider fasting and or abstaining from something. Fasting is not eating food for some time. Abstaining is temporarily not participating in pleasurable activities, such as Facebook, Instagram, etc.

> Isaiah 58:5-KJV Is this such a fast that I have chosen? A day for a man to afflict his soul? Is it to bow down his head as a bulrush, and to spread sackcloth and ashes under him? Wilt thou call this a fast, and an acceptable day to the Lord?

I will commit to fasting on

_____.

I will abstain from

_____.

"It's time to allow God to cut out the parts in our lives that consume us with feelings of hurt, betrayal, disappointment, bitterness, and hatred."

Chapter 4
Cut It Out

"For the wages of sin is death; but the gift of God is eternal life through Jesus Christ our Lord" - Romans 6:23 KJV

On July 1, 2016, I began my dream job as an elementary school principal. This was the moment I had been waiting for my whole life. I finally reached my goal. I was so excited! After working on the job for about seven months, I noticed that anytime I fasted I would have a pain in my stomach. I recall telling my husband that I needed to stop fasting because fasting was making my stomach hurt. He encouraged me to make an appointment with my doctor. I was thinking the pain was from the pregnancy of my youngest child. However, at my doctor's visit, she had ordered an ultrasound on my ovaries because of the area I described that the pain was coming from. I had the ultrasound and followed up with her two weeks later. I was told that everything was FINE. She asked, "Are you still having problems?" and I said I was. Before she finally let me go, she said, "Let me send you to a Gastrologist. You are too young for a colonoscopy, but we need to look at what is going on with your stomach." I had no worries; I assumed it was just stress from the job. She then scheduled the appointment, but I missed it. I was later reminded by a no-show bill of $75.00 that started an argument between my husband and I. He was upset, so I had to call and schedule another appointment. It was not with the same doctor.

At this point, I would have seen anyone just to get my husband off my back. After the colonoscopy, the doctor said he saw something on the other side of my stomach that was not in the area I had described the pain was coming from. He asked if I was having pain on my right side. I said, "No, it is at my bottom left." He said he had only seen something that would cause a mild irritation but ordered a biopsy anyway. It took about two weeks for the results to come back. When it finally did, I didn't like the look that was on his face, and I didn't like the feeling I was having. I must be totally honest; fear began to take over my thoughts. Questions filled my head. What if it is cancer and it has spread all over my body? What am I going to do? What will happen to my children? Who will take care of them? Will I lose my hair? Nevertheless, I kept telling myself I was going to be okay. The day came, and the doctor told my husband and I that the pathology results showed a benign tumor. TUMOR! He told us that it was going to have to be removed, but as to how soon was totally up to us. Tears began to roll down my face, and my mouth was glued shut. The thought of having a tumor inside of me even though the doctor said it was benign was devastating.

My husband asked who would be doing the surgery. The doctor said that he would be referring me to someone local. I really didn't want someone local to do my surgery. I wanted to go to UNC-Chapel Hill. UNC-Chapel Hill is a hospital that is famous for high quality patient care. They also have the most up to date equipment. I knew God had heard my unspoken request when the nurse came back and told my husband and I that the doctor changed his mind about sending me to "someone local". He wanted me to go to UNC-Chapel Hill. Don't tell me God doesn't answer before you call. Yet, the pain of doubt and unbelief flooded my mind. The next day, UNC-Chapel Hill sent my registration packet. When I opened it and read the words "Cancer Center," my heart dropped. Why am I going to a Cancer Center if it is a benign tumor? Is this more serious what the doctor told me?

My husband was not able to go with me to my first doctor's visit, so I called one of my best friends, and she took the trip with me. During that appointment, the doctor broke the news that it was not a benign tumor, and it may have already spread. I looked at my friend; little did she know I was fasting and praying that a miracle would take place and all of this would be over. She looked at me as if my faith was strong and asked, "Why are you crying?" I started contemplating if I missed a scripture on how to respond to terrible news. I couldn't control my tears. How do I explain to my colleagues and family that I have cancer and need to have surgery?

With the help of the Lord, I got through it. I remember my husband trying to make me have a level of Faith that I did not have at the time. I felt he wanted me to believe the way he was believing. I wasn't there. This later caused problems between us because the enemy led me to think that he did not understand what I was going through. Almost everyone I shared my news with had the same response, "It's okay, just trust God." I now understand that they just didn't know what to say.

I had a successful surgery, thanks to the prayers of the saints. After coming home, I remembered sitting on the couch crying and asking God why He allowed this to happen to me. He said, "If you had not forgiven your father, you would have died with this cancer." When I went for my follow-up appointment, the confirmation came. The doctor told me that the pathology report showed that I had these tumors for a while. "How do you know?" I asked. He explained that the type of tumor I had takes years to develop and grows very slowly. This type of cancer is called Neuroendocrine, also known as NETs.

A neuroendocrine tumor may grow slowly or aggressively and spread to other parts of the body. Many people do not develop symptoms, and the tumor is detected incidentally. When they occur, they can vary based on the location of the tumor. They are normally found in the digestive system, lungs, and most common, the pancreas. The most common NET symptoms are abdominal pain, flushing, diarrhea, wheezing, bloating, and heart palpitation. In rare cases, skin flushing or fluctuating blood sugar levels may occur. 1 My team of doctors were all puzzled as to how I found out. I had to explain to them several times that I didn't have the symptoms they kept asking me about.

Please, if you don't get anything else out of this book, let go of any unforgiveness that you may be holding on to! The cancer had spread to three of my lymph nodes. However, I did not need any radiation or chemotherapy.

Today, I have the scars to remind me to walk in love and forgiveness. It's hard, but it's a choice. The enemy tried to make me angry after my surgery against friends, family members, and church members who did not reach out to me when I was down. God allowed all the right people to visit me at that time. When I started to get upset about those who I expected to come and were not there, I quickly looked down at my stomach to see the scars and it reminded me to let it go!

Listen to what research says about unforgiveness on your health: Unforgiveness is classified in medical books as a disease. According to Dr. Steven Staniford, chief of surgery at the Cancer Treatment Centers of America, refusing to forgive makes people sick and keeps them that way. It was also shocking to read that 61% of cancer patients have forgiveness issues, according to Dr. Michael Barry.2

It's not that unforgiveness causes cancer. It's that the suppression of anger, resentment, and grief disrupts the normal operation of our bodies. These disruptions can lead to a weakened immune system. Therefore, when the immune system is weak, it opens the doors to illnesses and diseases.

It's time…. It's time to allow God to cut out the parts of our lives that consume us with feelings of hurt, betrayal, disappointment, bitterness, and hatred. Let Him do it! Do not let those things spread. They will spread, just like the cancer that was in my body. But you can allow God to cut them out! When God does the cutting, He knows how to sew you up so the scar will be faint and only serve as a reminder.

Reflection of Chapter 4
Cut It Out

Please feel free to write your response below or in a journal. Ask yourself the following question:

What are you taking away from my experience with unforgiveness?

_____
_____
_____
_____
_____
_____
_____
_____
_____
_____
_____
_____
_____
_____
_____
_____

"When you are angry, it is hard to think rationally."

Chapter 5
Are You Roaming?

"And the world is passing away along with its desires, but whoever does the will of God abides forever." - 1 John 2:17 - ESV

One day, I had to go out of town to attend a workshop for school principals. I left certain people in charge because my assistant principal was going to be off campus, as well. There was a huge field trip planned for all of our fourth-graders. I remember calling my boss to have all my bases covered just in case something happened at school. After sitting in the workshop for half an hour, I received a text message stating that the 4th-grade students had loaded the buses for the trip. However, forty-five minutes later, I got an email that said that the field trip is canceled. My heart began to race. I immediately got up in the middle of the meeting to go outside in the parking lot and call the school. In my angry voice I asked, "WHO CANCELLED THE FIELD TRIP?" I asked again because the person who answered the phone did not say anything. Then, she told me she didn't know, but there were parents in the office, and several calls were coming in. So, I hung up to call the person I left in charge. Every time I dialed the number, I heard a recording which said, "You are roaming. Please contact your service provider for local customer care." So, I moved to another area in the parking lot and dialed again. The message again said, "You are roaming. Please contact your service provider for local customer service." So, I proceeded to move to another area because I

I received the same message again! I was mad. Then, the Holy Spirit spoke. "You are roaming, not just with your phone. You are in a position I can't cover you. You will have to pay for this one. When you roam spiritually, you wander outside of your covered zone, which is, God's perfect Will."

During this time in my life, I was dealing with leading a school, helping my husband pastor a church, and wanting to be the best mom I could possibly be. With all these added stressors, I constantly ran low on patience. I found myself saying whatever I felt like saying based on how I felt in the moment. After all, I felt I let down the kids who were looking forward to this field trip. I know now that I can't go back to how I used to deal with people. God can't cover me with an unfiltered angry tone towards others. The Bible says, "My dear brothers and sisters, take note of this: Everyone should be quick to listen, slow to speak and slow to become angry, because human anger does not produce the righteousness that God desires." James 1:19-20 (NIV)

In the situation at school, I attacked the people and not the issue. Often when you get angry, you will attack the person and not the issues at hand. The solution is found in His Word: "A gentle answer turns away wrath, but a harsh word stirs up anger." Proverbs 15:1 (NIV) I calmed down and was able to get my emotions together. I went inside the building to ask if I could use the phone because I needed to call my school. The receptionist cleared a conference room for me where I could sit with no distractions. When you are angry, it is hard to think rationally. I wasted all that time in the parking lot, and all had to do was calm down and ask someone if I could use the phone.

God has a plan for us, just like Verizon, Sprint, T-Mobile, and Boost. When we roam outside of the plan that God has designed, it becomes sin. We are going to give an account for the sins we have committed. Anger is not the only area that is not covered in God's plan. God's plan does not cover us when we are, cheating, stealing, walking in disobedience, and doing things that defile our bodies. These things separate us from our service provider. It is impossible to get a prayer through when you are roaming. You can't call on Him; it's like talking while on mute. Your prayers are not being heard. "If I regard iniquity in my heart the Lord will not hear me." Psalms 66:18 (KJV)

So, you may be asking what this has to do with unforgiveness. Well, a lot! I spent so many years roaming and blaming my dad for the things he had done; I didn't consider that I needed forgiveness myself. The Bible says, "For all have sinned and fallen short of the glory of God." Who am I not to forgive when I stand in need of so much forgiveness myself? The Lord knows me, and He knows how anger will keep me from my destiny. Therefore, He has allowed situations to come that required my forgiveness. So, how do I follow the plan of God? How do I keep myself from roaming?

Chip Ingram, (one of my favorite ministers) shared his ABCD's practical ways to deal with anger. Anger is not the problem, it is the warning light that something is wrong. Therefore, you must do the following:

A-Acknowledge - I recognize why I am angry. Is it disappointment, hurt, frustration, guilt, shame, etc.?

B-Back-track to the primary emotion - I acknowledge how I feel. "I feel _____." (attack the issue, not the person).

C-Consider the real cause - Why are you feeling this way?

D-Determine the right response. Confront the offender. How will you deal with it? Speak the truth in love. (Email, Call, or have a Face-to-Face meeting)

If you are found in the wrong:

Repent - Live a life of repentance. I am nowhere near perfect. I am always repenting because I desire to please God.

Ask - Acknowledge the person you have hurt and ask them to forgive you.

Listen - Allow them time to explain. Even though the offense wasn't intentional does not mean the hurt isn't real.

Seek - Peace and move on!

Reflection of Chapter 5
Are you Roaming?

Please feel free to write your response below or in a journal. Ask yourself the following questions:

Take a moment to reflect. Are you in a place where God can cover you? If you answered "no," explain why.

_____
_____
_____
_____
_____
_____
_____
_____
_____
_____
_____
_____
_____
_____
_____
_____

Read the following scripture. What does this mean to you?

"For the anger of man does not produce the righteousness of God." James 1:20 (ESV)

"One of the hardest things you will ever have to do is forgive the people who should have been there when they were not."

Chapter 6
Copy Me

"Don't copy the behavior and customs of this world, but let God transform you into a new person by changing the way you think."
- Romans 12:2 - NLT

We live in a world filled with imperfect people. Therefore, it's hard to go through life if you don't know how to forgive others. In this chapter, you will discover how important it is to copy God! We've covered a lot of ground. It is my prayer that by the time you get through this chapter, you will be ready to obey God's Word, no matter what!

When life is going well, it's easy to see the truth of His Word, but when we are overtaken by difficulties, what do we do? Jesus tells His disciples in Matthew 16:24, "If anyone would come after me, let him deny himself and take up his cross and follow me." Following Jesus when you're battling with anger, bitterness, and unforgiveness is not easy. You don't want to carry that cross; you want to throw the cross at the person causing all of the hurt, pain, and disappointment.

There is another passage in the Bible where Jesus was in the Garden of Gethsemane. He was at the most crucial moment of His life on Earth. He wanted His friends to be there and support Him. He knew they could not help Him, but He just wanted their support. Unfortunately, they disappointed Him and fell asleep, but He didn't hold it against them. One of the hardest things you will ever do is forgive the people who should have been there when they were not. Anger is not the problem. Anger is like the red warning light on your dashboard. When a person becomes angry, it means something is wrong under the hood. It could be disappointment, hurt, jealousy, shame, depression, or embarrassment. Please note anger is a secondary emotion.

There is another passage of scripture where Jesus is turning the tables over in the temple. It shows that God can identify with our emotions, too. He knows exactly what we are going through. Ephesians 4:26 says, "In your anger do not sin, do not let the sun go down on your wrath." When you don't deal with your anger, it will lead to sin, and when sin is conceived, it will bring forth death. Death is not always physical; you can die spiritually and emotionally.

The Lord just wants us to COPY HIM. Commit to memorizing this 3-step process: Choose to forgive, go through the process of forgiving, and then walk in forgiveness

The 3 Step Process of Forgiveness

1. **Forgiveness is a Choice.** You may not feel like it, but you can choose not to hold on to the offense.

2. **Forgiveness is a Process.** This process begins with prayer. Your prayers may not sound good at first, but keep praying. God will help you as you give the issues of your heart to Him. During this process, you will do something good for the offender.

3. **Forgiveness is Continual.** You know you have forgiven when you experience joy when good things happen in the offender's life and you are genuinely happy for them. During this stage you also realize that you need forgiveness when you fall short.

You may say, "I have followed those steps, but the person keeps hurting me!" The Bible tells us this in Matthew 18:21-22, "Then Peter came to Jesus and asked, "Lord, how many times shall I forgive my brother or sister who sins against me? Up to seven times?" Jesus answered, "I tell you, not seven times, but seventy-seven times." Let's make a choice to Copy HIM.

Reflection of Chapter 6
Copy Me

Please feel free to write your response below or in a journal. Ask yourself the following questions:

After reading this chapter, what is something you can begin applying today?

_____

_____

_____

_____

_____

_____

_____

_____

_____

_____

_____

_____

_____

_____

_____

_____

_____

If the person keeps hurting you after you have forgiven them, what will you do?

_____

_____

_____

_____

_____

_____

_____

_____

_____

_____

What does the Bible tell us about how many times to forgive someone? Elaborate. What does that mean to you?

_____

_____

_____

_____

_____

_____

_____

_____

_____

_____

"Forgiveness is not just about saying words. It is an active process in which you make a conscious decision to let go of negative feelings whether the person deserves it or not."

Chapter 7
Married, Single, or Divorced: FORGIVE

Love is patient, love is kind. It does not envy, it does not boast, it is not proud. It does not dishonor others, it is not self-seeking, it is not easily angered, it keeps no record of wrongs.
-I Corinthians 13:4-5 - NIV

If you are married, FORGIVE. If you are single, FORGIVE. If you are divorced, FORGIVE. Forgiveness is not just about saying the words. "It is an active process in which you make a conscious decision to let go of negative feelings whether the person deserves it or not."3 Karen Swartz, M.D., says, "As you release the anger, resentment, and hostility, you begin to feel empathy, compassion, and sometimes even affection for the person who wronged you." Remember, when we do not address issues that hurt us, we bury the things that we should confront.

I remember my Pastor telling me during one of my counseling sessions that I would not be ready for marriage if I did not forgive. Little did I know that he was so RIGHT! In my ten years of marriage, I think I have had to choose to forgive my husband every week for something. I do it because I need forgiveness when I mess up, too. I also want to remain healthy both inside and out.

Like with my parents, if your spouse had an affair, recognize that the affair is not a reflection of your worth. Forgive, and if you can work it out, please do. If you want your marriage, fight for it. I strongly recommend counseling! I know several marriages that have survived after an affair, but it took work from both parties and God.

Now that I have children, it is clear to me that if I had continued the path of unforgiveness, they would have to fight a generational curse. I do not wish such harm on my children; therefore, I must live a life of forgiveness and teach them to do the same. When I look back over my life, I recall relationships that I was in as a single adult. I remember my heart being broken by men who said they loved me. I remember thinking that I was their only one to later find I wasn't.

As a single man or woman, forgive and move on. It does not mean that you return to the relationship; rather, it is releasing those toxic feelings. Stop now if you are guilty of this and REPENT! I know for a fact this can be done. I watched my mother model forgiveness before my eyes even after her divorce. She got to the point in her life where she just had to move on. Because of her relationship with God, she can communicate with my father and his wife with nothing negative in her heart. It bothers me when I see Christian couples who have divorced and can't speak or hold adult conversations. It also bothers me when a mother or father speaks negatively about the other parent in front of their children. This type of behavior only adds to the problem.

Remember, God is with you. He promised in His Word that He would never leave us nor forsake us. He will be right there to heal every part of our bodies and emotions that hurt. A recent study showed that people whose forgiveness came from understanding that no one is perfect were able to resume a normal relationship with the other person, even if that person never apologized. The choice is simple; Let it Go or Die with It!

Reflection of Chapter 7
Married, Single, Divorced

Please feel free to write your response below or in a journal. Ask yourself the following questions:

<u>Married</u>: Is there tension between you and your spouse? Why?

_____

_____

_____

<u>Single</u>: Do you still have unresolved anger from a past relationship? Why?

_____

_____

_____

<u>Divorce</u>: Can you hold a conversation with your ex? If not, why?

_____

_____

_____

_____

If you are Married, Single, or Divorced _____.
(fill in the blank)

"We must give credit to the Word of God for drawing us closer to him and not Satan's attacks."

A word from the *Word*

Walking in unforgiveness will block your prayers. It will block your ability to flow in the things of God. Read the following scriptures to discover how God feels about us holding on to offenses, resentment, and bitterness.

"I have hidden your word in my heart that I might not sin against you." **Psalm 119:11 (NIV)**

"Be ye angry, and sin not: let not the sun go down upon your wrath:" **Ephesians 4:26 (KJV)**

"And when ye stand praying, forgive, if ye have ought against any: that your Father also which is in heaven may forgive you your trespasses." **Mark 11: 25 (KJV)**

"For if ye forgive men their trespasses, your heavenly Father will also forgive you: But if ye forgive not men their trespasses, neither will your Father forgive your trespasses." **Matthew 6:14-15 (KJV)**

"He that saith he is in the light, and hateth his brother, is in darkness even until now. He that loveth his brother abideth in the light, and there is none occasion of stumbling in him. But he that hateth his brother is in darkness, and walketh in darkness, and knoweth not whither he goeth, because that darkness hath blinded his eyes." I **John 2:9-11 (KJV)**

"If a man says, I love God, and hateth his brother, he is a liar: for he that loveth not his brother whom he hath seen, how can he love God whom he hath not seen? And this commandment have we from him, that he who loveth God love his brother also." I **John 4:20-21 (KJV)**

"If a man says, I love God, and hateth his brother, he is a liar: for he that loveth not his brother whom he hath seen, how can he love God whom he hath not seen? And this commandment have we from him, that he who loveth God love his brother also." I John 4:20-21 (KJV) When words are many, sin is not absent, but he who holds his tongue is wise. **Proverbs 10:19 (NIV)**

He who guards his lips guards his life, but he who speaks rashly will come to ruin. **Proverbs 13:3 (NIV)**

Do you see a man who speaks in haste? There is more hope for a fool than for him. **Proverbs 29:20 (NIV)**

Prayer Journal

Now that you have completed this book. I must warn you that an attack will come! The enemy will do whatever he can to keep you in bondage to bitterness and unforgiveness. I have included a prayer journal to guide you through the process of forgiveness each time an offense may occur. Included, are a series of questions that will assist you in getting to the root of your problem. Be totally honest with yourself and more importantly with God!

It's time to

Pray!

Prayer Journal

"I pour out my complaint before him,
I reveal my trouble to him." Psalms 142:2

Confess your pain. What words or actions hurt you the most?

What do you need God to do?
Tell Him.

How will you handle your feelings?
(disappointment, shame, embarrassment,
confusion, jealousy, fear, etc.)

List the scripture or scriptures you will apply to the situation.

As a result of your prayer: What is God saying? What is He telling you to do?

I choose life!

Prayer Journal

"I pour out my complaint before him,
I reveal my trouble to him." Psalms 142:2

Confess your pain. What words or actions hurt you the most?

What do you need God to do?
Tell Him.

How will you handle your feelings?
(disappointment, shame, embarrassment,
confusion, jealousy, fear, etc.)

List the scripture or scriptures you will apply
to the situation.

As a result of your prayer: What is God saying? What is He telling you to do?

I will live!

Prayer Journal

"I pour out my complaint before him,
I reveal my trouble to him." Psalms 142:2

Confess your pain. What words or actions hurt you the most?

What do you need God to do? Tell Him.

How will you handle your feelings? (disappointment, shame, embarrassment, confusion, jealousy, fear, etc.)

_____

_____

_____

_____

_____

_____

_____

_____

_____

_____

_____

_____

_____

_____

_____

_____

_____

_____

List the scripture or scriptures you will apply to the situation.

_____
_____
_____
_____
_____
_____
_____
_____
_____
_____
_____
_____
_____
_____
_____
_____
_____
_____
_____
_____

As a result of your prayer: What is God saying? What is He telling you to do?

Forgiveness = Life

Prayer Journal

"I pour out my complaint before him,
I reveal my trouble to him." Psalms 142:2

Confess your pain. What words or actions hurt you the most?

_____
_____
_____
_____
_____
_____
_____
_____
_____
_____
_____
_____
_____
_____
_____
_____
_____

What do you need God to do?
Tell Him.

How will you handle your feelings?
(disappointment, shame, embarrassment,
confusion, jealousy, fear, etc.)

List the scripture or scriptures you will apply to the situation.

_____

_____

_____

_____

_____

_____

_____

_____

_____

_____

_____

_____

_____

_____

_____

_____

_____

_____

_____

_____

_____

As a result of your prayer: What is God saying? What is He telling you to do?

I choose to forgive!

Prayer Journal

"I pour out my complaint before him,
I reveal my trouble to him." Psalms 142:2

Confess your pain. What words or actions hurt you the most?

_____

_____

_____

_____

_____

_____

_____

_____

_____

_____

_____

_____

_____

_____

_____

_____

_____

_____

_____

What do you need God to do?
Tell Him.

How will you handle your feelings?
(disappointment, shame, embarrassment,
confusion, jealousy, fear, etc.)

List the scripture or scriptures you will apply
to the situation.

As a result of your prayer: What is God saying? What is He telling you to do?

_____

_____

_____

_____

_____

_____

_____

_____

_____

_____

_____

_____

_____

_____

_____

_____

_____

_____

_____

Forgiveness
is a process!

Prayer Journal

"I pour out my complaint before him,
I reveal my trouble to him." Psalms 142:2

Confess your pain. What words or actions hurt you the most?

What do you need God to do?
Tell Him.

How will you handle your feelings?
(disappointment, shame, embarrassment,
confusion, jealousy, fear, etc.)

List the scripture or scriptures you will apply
to the situation.

_____

_____

_____

_____

_____

_____

_____

_____

_____

_____

_____

_____

_____

_____

_____

_____

_____

_____

_____

_____

As a result of your prayer: What is God saying? What is He telling you to do?

There is freedom in forgiveness!

Prayer Journal

"I pour out my complaint before him,
I reveal my trouble to him." Psalms 142:2

Confess your pain. What words or actions hurt you the most?

What do you need God to do?
Tell Him.

How will you handle your feelings?
(disappointment, shame, embarrassment,
confusion, jealousy, fear, etc.)

List the scripture or scriptures you will apply
to the situation.

As a result of your prayer: What is God saying? What is He telling you to do?

_____
_____
_____
_____
_____
_____
_____
_____
_____
_____
_____
_____
_____
_____
_____
_____
_____
_____

I let go of

unforgiveness!

Final Thoughts

Please note, I am not an expert on forgiveness. As I was writing this book, people resurfaced that I needed to forgive all over again. However, I am not the same person. I choose to FORGIVE! It is my prayer that this book has helped you learn how to as well. After having my surgery, I can honestly say that my quality of life has improved. I strive to be more active and enjoy my life. I continue to identify my triggers in the area of forgiveness as I continue to lead in my home, job, church, and community. Challenges may come but, now I know that I must forgive to live. Please consider passing this book along to someone you feel may benefit from reading it.

Acknowledgments

I acknowledge God, who is first in my life and who inspired me to write this book.

I acknowledge my grandparents, who always supported my family until their deaths, Talbert & Edna Mae Cox.

I acknowledge my mother, Sharon Holmes, father Jimmie Cox, Papa David (Step-Dad) and Audrey Cox (Step-Mom) for all their support and encouragement.

I acknowledge my spiritual mother and father, Pastor Earl & Denise Goings, without whom, I would have died with unforgiveness in my heart. Words cannot express how grateful I am that you did not give up on me.

I acknowledge and humbly thank my husband, Victor McEachern, for allowing me to take your time and devote myself to writing this book.
I acknowledge my children, Victor McEachern II and Erin Milan McEachern. Thank you both for helping me to be the best mother I can be. Erin, thanks for reminding me to get off Instagram and write my book.

I acknowledge and humbly thank my brother, Jimmie Cox Jr., and sister-in-law, Stephanie Cox, for being a part of this journey.

I acknowledge my sisters, Eretta, Debinee, Laquita, Twanda, and Shaquita who keep me on my knees; I love all of you unconditionally. I acknowledge my special sisters, Erika White, Renee Richardson, Latoya Grace, Taurus Tyson, and Deidrea Cox who helped pray me through this trying time in my life.

I acknowledge two special couples who I admire dearly. Elder Milton & Marie Ann Guions and Raymond & Roxanne Henely. You never gave up on me and supported me in every season of my life.

I acknowledge my big sister Louise Sellars. All I had to do was call and tell you what to pray for; good, bad, and ugly. After you corrected me, you prayed and loved me through it.

I acknowledge all my nieces and nephews who I feel like I birthed; I love you guys to life and only want the BEST for you!

I acknowledge Terrenique Leadon for coaching me through this process. Your support has truly been a blessing in my life.

I acknowledge Vander Williams who has encouraged me from the very beginning of this journey. You have truly made a difference in my life.

I acknowledge Ebony Bailey for the push, the prayers, the deliverance session, the truth, and for being my voice of reasoning. I know that you are God-sent. May God continue to bless you for the seeds you have sown into my life.

I acknowledge Dr. Andrea K. Dickerson M.D., for providing me with quality health care through every season in my life. All because you listened, I was able to find these tumors early. Thanks for always listening!

NOTES

1.   Forgiveness Definition: What Is Forgiveness. (2020). https://greatergood.berkeley.edu/topic/forgiveness /definition.

2.   Forgiveness: Your Health Depends on It. | Johns Hopkins Medicine. https://www.hopkinsmedicine.org/health/wellness-and-prevention/forgiveness-your-health-depends-on-it

3.   What Is NET Cancer and Where Does NETs Occur On The Body? Neuroendocrine Cancer Awareness Network. https://www.netcancerawareness.org/what-is-net-cancer/

STAY CONNECTED

Instagram
@theleadinggem

Facebook
/gemettemceachern

Twitter
@GemetteM

Email
theleadinggem@gmail.com

Made in the USA
Columbia, SC
11 November 2021

48794878R00063